SLIM GOODBODY'S

Fabulous Fruits

CRABTREE
Publishing Company
www.crabtreebooks.com

Crabtree Publishing Company
www.crabtreebooks.com

Series development, writing, and packaging:
John Burstein, Slim Goodbody Corp.

Editors:
Molly Aloian
Reagan Miller
Mark Sachner, Water Buffalo Books

Editorial director:
Kathy Middleton

Production coordinator:
Kenneth Wright

Prepress technician:
Kenneth Wright

Designer:
Tammy West, Westgraphix LLC

Photos:
Chris Pinchback, Pinchback Photography

Photo credits:
© Slim Goodbody, iStockphotos, and Shutterstock images.

"Slim Goodbody" and Pinchback photos, copyright,
© Slim Goodbody

Acknowledgements:
The author would like to thank the following people for
their help in this project:
Christine Burstein, Olivia Davis, Kylie Fong, Nathan Levig,
Havana Lyman, Andrew McBride, Lulu McClure, Ben
McGinnis, Esme Power, Joe Ryan

"Slim Goodbody" and "Slim Goodbody's Nutrition Edition"
are registered trademarks of the Slim Goodbody Corp.

Library and Archives Canada Cataloguing in Publication

Burstein, John
      Fabulous fruits / John Burstein.

(Slim Goodbody's nutrition edition)
Includes index.
ISBN 978-0-7787-5042-0 (bound).--ISBN 978-0-7787-5057-4 (pbk.)

      1. Fruit in human nutrition--Juvenile literature. 2. Nutrition--Juvenile
literature. I. Title. II. Series:°Burstein, John. Slim Goodbody's nutrition
edition.

QP144.F78B87 2010   j641.3'4   C2009-903854-4

Library of Congress Cataloging-in-Publication Data

Burstein, John.
    Fabulous fruits / John Burstein.
       p. cm. -- (Slim Goodbody's nutrition edition)
    Includes index.
    ISBN 978-0-7787-5042-0 (reinforced lib. bdg. : alk. paper) -- ISBN 978-0-
7787-5057-4 (pbk. : alk. paper)
    1. Fruit in human nutrition--Juvenile literature. 2. Nutrition--Juvenile
literature. 3. Children--Nutrition--Requirements--Juvenile literature. I. Title.
II. Series.

    QP144.F78B87 2010
    641.3'4--dc22

                                                           2009024560

Crabtree Publishing Company
www.crabtreebooks.com   1-800-387-7650

Published in Canada
Crabtree Publishing
616 Welland Ave.
St. Catharines, Ontario
L2M 5V6

Published in the United States
Crabtree Publishing
PMB16A
350 Fifth Ave., Suite 3308
New York, NY 10118

Published in the United Kingdom
Crabtree Publishing
White Cross Mills
High Town, Lancaster
LA1 4XS

Published in Australia
Crabtree Publishing
386 Mt. Alexander Rd.
Ascot Vale (Melbourne)
VIC 3032

Contents

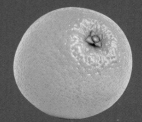

GREETINGS

My name is Slim Goodbody.
I want to ask you two questions.

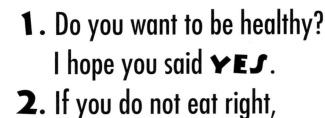

1. Do you want to be healthy?
I hope you said **YES**.

2. If you do not eat right,
can you be healthy?
I hope you said **NO**.

The food pyramid helps you eat right.

There are six stripes on the U.S. food pyramid.

The stripes stand for the five different food groups plus oils.

GRAINS
VEGETABLES
FRUITS
OILS
MILK
MEAT
& BEANS

This book is about the fruit food group.

FRUITS!

Fruits belong on the red stripe in the U.S. food pyramid. Fruits come in many colors.

grapes

kiwi

apple

plums

grapes

Each color is good for you.

cherries

watermelon

strawberry

blueberries

cantaloupe

orange

apricot

banana

lemon

pineapple

Try to eat fruits of every color each week.

All Fruits are Plants

Every fruit comes from a plant. Different kinds of fruits come from different kinds of plants.

Some fruits grow on trees.

Plants give us a lot of fruits.

Some fruits grow on small plants.

Some fruits grow on bushes.

Some fruits grow on vines.

AROUND THE WORLD

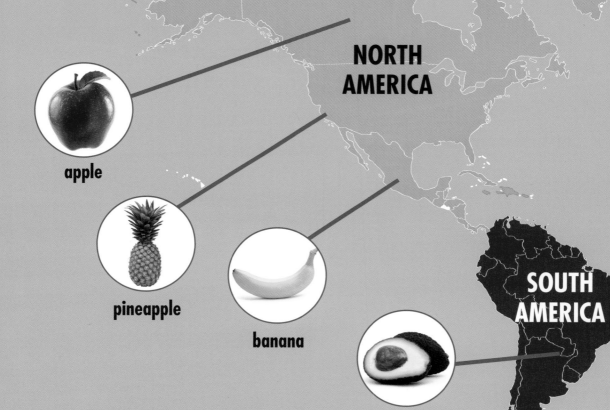

apple

pineapple

banana

avocado

NORTH AMERICA

SOUTH AMERICA

Fruits grow all around the world.

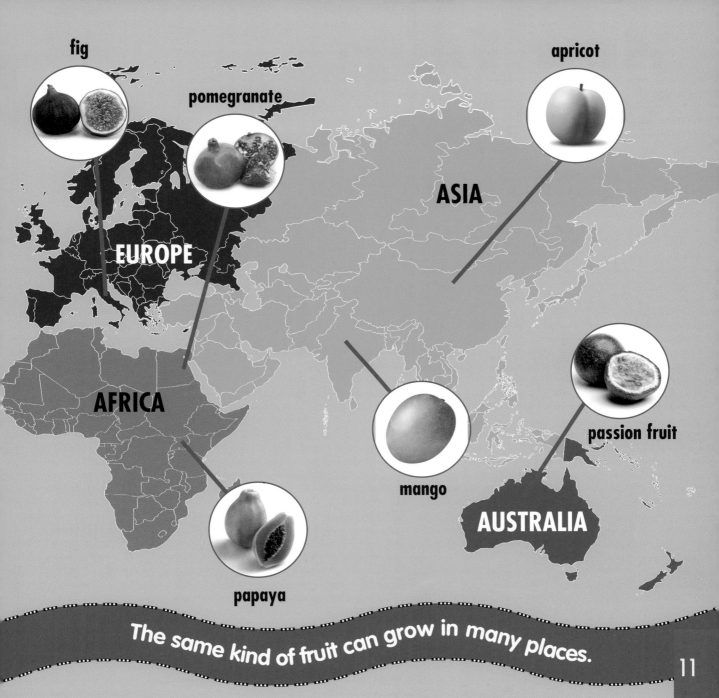

fig

pomegranate

apricot

ASIA

EUROPE

AFRICA

passion fruit

mango

AUSTRALIA

papaya

The same kind of fruit can grow in many places.

How Fruit Travels

Fruits may come from faraway places.

When fruit arrives aboard a ship
Or flies in on a plane,
The fruit is taken off and loaded
On a railroad train.

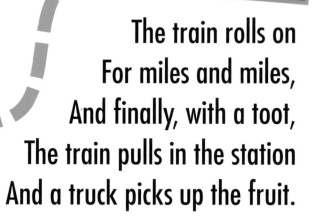

The train rolls on
For miles and miles,
And finally, with a toot,
The train pulls in the station
And a truck picks up the fruit.

Think about how fruit travels to get to you.

The truck drives to a store and then
The fruit gets carried in.
Later on your parents see it
Stacked inside a bin.

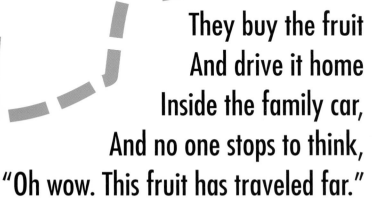

They buy the fruit
And drive it home
Inside the family car,
And no one stops to think,
"Oh wow. This fruit has traveled far."

So next time that you take a bite
And think a fruit tastes yummy,
Remember all the miles it took
To reach your hungry tummy!

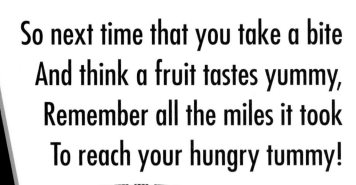

Less Pollution

Planes, ships, trucks, and cars use fuel. Fuel gives them energy to move.

Fuel also puts pollution in the air.

The less food has to travel, the less fuel is used. Less fuel means less air pollution.

Try to buy foods that are grown near where you live. Sometimes local farmers bring their foods to town. They sell their foods at "farmers'" markets. Many stores also sell food from local farms.

Buying food at farmers' markets is good for the Earth.

FRUITS KEEP YOU HEALTHY

Fruits help you stay healthy.

Some fruits help your heart stay strong.

Some fruits help your brain work well.

Some fruits help your eyes see well.

Some fruits help your bones and muscles stay strong.

Some fruits help you stay healthy by fighting germs.

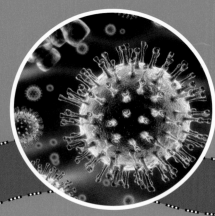

Fruits help different body parts.

Fruits You Need Each Day

You need to eat 1½ cups (375 ml) of fruit every day.

You can use these two lists to help you get the fruit you need. Each day, eat something from the ONE CUP LIST and something from the ½ CUP LIST.

Feel free to mix and match the fruits any way you like.

ONE CUP LIST

8 large strawberries
1 slice of watermelon
1 small apple
1 medium orange
1 mango
1 medium grapefruit
1 large banana
32 grapes
1 pear
2 canned peach halves
1 cup of 100% orange juice

1/2 CUP LIST

16 grapes
1/2 large banana
4 large strawberries
1/2 pear
1/2 glass of orange juice
1 small container of applesauce
1 large plum
1/2 small apple
1/2 orange
1/2 mango
1/2 grapefruit

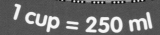

1 cup = 250 ml   1/2 cup = 125 ml

Almost any time is a good time to eat fruit.

Fruits are good for you.

You can have bananas on your cereal for breakfast.

You can drink a glass of apple juice with lunch.

You can snack on an apple after school.

You can eat strawberries with ice cream for dessert.

Fruits taste great!

WORLD FOOD GUIDES

The U.S. food pyramid is only one guide to eating well.

To learn more about Canada's Food Guide, check out the Web site below.

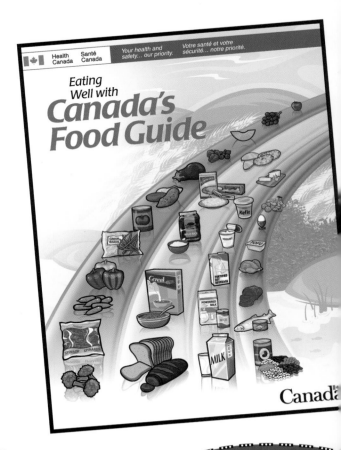

www.nms.on.ca/Elementary/canada.htm

People from different parts of the world often eat different kinds of foods. People use different food guides to help them eat wisely.

Words to Know

 **avocado**

 **bin**

 **cantaloupe**

 **germs**

 **kiwi**

 **pomegranate**

Find Out More

Books

Oliver's Fruit Salad, Vivian French (Author), Alison Bartlett (Illustrator), Orchard Books

A Fruit Is a Suitcase for Seeds, Jean Richards (Author), Anca Hariton (Illustrator), First Avenue Editions

Web Sites

MyPyramid.gov
www.mypyramid.gov/kids/index.html

Slim Goodbody
www.slimgoodbody.com

Printed in the U.S.A.-CG